FENG SHUI
CURES

FENG SHUI
CURES

Using the practical tools and
remedies of feng shui

Antonia Beattie

BARNES
&NOBLE
BOOKS
NEW YORK

Contents

What Are Feng Shui Cures? 6

Useful feng shui cures: the eight main categories • Attracting positive energy by using feng shui cures • Choosing the right cure to deflect negative energy • Using a cure to maximum effect

A–Z of Feng Shui Cures 14

Animal symbols • Artwork • Bagua • Bells • Birds and other creatures that fly • Candles • Coins • Color • Crystals • Curtains • Elements (Earth, Fire, Metal, Water, Wood) • Fish tanks • Floor rugs • Flutes • Fruit • Furniture • Hedges • Insects • Lamps and lighting • Mirrors • Mobiles • Pets • Plants • Scatter cushions • Screens • Sounds • Statues • Water features • Wind chimes

Using Feng Shui Cures 48

MONEY 48

Attracting wealth and prosperity • Keeping hold of money • Encouraging success in business

What Are Feng Shui Cures?

Useful feng shui cures: the eight main categories

The belief that underpins the ancient Chinese art of feng shui is that we are surrounded by an invisible life force that flows and eddies around and through us, and that it is possible to manipulate this energy for our benefit.

Feng shui is an extremely effective way of improving the flow of beneficial energy within your home. The way this energy flows around your house or office has a marked influence on whether you experience relationship problems, poor finances, or blocks in your career or education.

If the energy becomes blocked or stagnant, or is made to move too fast, it turns into a negative force that can cause all manner of problems in your life. There are a number of different techniques for blocking or dispersing negative energy. One of these is the use of feng shui cures or remedies.

Feng shui cures are either easy-to-obtain objects or simple concepts that we can all use and integrate in the space around us and our families or workplaces. There are eight major types of feng shui cures:

* color
* reflective objects, such as lights, mirrors, and crystals
* harmonious sounds of wind chimes and bells
* plants and pets
* mobiles and flags
* statues and rocks
* fans and flutes
* electrical or mechanical objects.

These types of cures are called "chushi" cures. Chushi cures are objects that can be added to a space to improve the flow of energy there. There are other types of cures, called "rushi" cures, which involve more heavy-duty changes, such as installing a window in a windowless room or removing a load-bearing wall. Such solutions are sometimes not practical or economical – chushi cures are usually an equally effective substitute.

In this book, we will show you how to use various feng shui cures and where to place them in your home or office for maximum effect. You usually only need one or two feng shui cures to make a difference in how your home feels and gain some improvement in your life. Use your intuition to help you choose the right cure for you.

Many of the cures that we discuss in this book will fit easily into any decor, not just oriental-style interiors. Feng shui cures are easy and fun and can make a dramatic difference in your life.

Attracting positive energy by using feng shui cures

We know instinctively when positive energy is flowing around us. Opportunities come our way without effort; we receive thoughtful, caring help when we need it; and we achieve a great deal in terms of our studies and career. These are some of the indications that we are living in a home where positive energy is flowing around us.

If people comment on how comfortable and pleasant it is to visit your home or feel that excellent results occur after a meeting at your workplace, this is a further indication that positive or beneficial energy is flowing through your home or workplace and into your life.

The key to attracting positive energy is the introduction of harmony and balance into your space. In feng shui, harmony and balance are symbolized by the use of melodious sounds and attractive, pleasant images. Sometimes feng shui cures are introduced in pairs – for example, the placement of two ducks on a small round mirror is a symbol of luck in relationships.

Positive energy moves in curves, and is attracted to pieces of furniture that are curved and that do not have sharp corners. Round and oval tables or place mats encourage more harmonious dinner conversations than square or rectangular tables and place mats do.

Many feng shui cures involve rounded edges. For example, if choosing a mirror, it is important to make sure that it is one that is rounded or is within a curved frame. Usually, plants used as a feng shui cure should have rounded leaves or flowers.

Balance is very important in feng shui, and is symbolized in the yin/yang symbol, which indicates the fundamental duality of life – male and female, light and dark. Yin is passive energy and is symbolized as dark colors and space, while yang is aggressive energy and is represented by light, bright colors and objects.

Feng shui cures often include adding bright, golden colors to a room to encourage the flow of positive energy into it. It is important that the feng shui cure does not create an imbalance in the energy of the room. For example, too much bright color in a space may create excessive yang energy – a person who constantly uses the room may experience restlessness and headaches. Balance is the key to using feng shui cures.

Choosing the right cure
to deflect negative energy

If life seems too hard or just plain frustrating, it may be that you are inadvertently attracting negative energy. In feng shui, the energy that is allowed to naturally flow around us is always considered positive or beneficial. For example, we often feel rejuvenated and invigorated after we have had a walk (in a natural environment) or a swim (in a fresh, bubbling stream or the ocean).

Negative energy is also created in nature – earthquakes, jagged mountain peaks, and volcanoes are examples. Humankind has created negative energy by the injudicious placement of sharp-angled objects and long, straight tunnels, including such things as power lines, poles, tunnels and straight roads, as well as rooflines, long corridors, and L-shaped rooms.

Rooms shaped so that there is a corner protruding into the space, and rooflines aimed at a section of your home or office, are believed to create "poison arrows," which are lines of fast-moving energy that can create negative energy in your life. The first indication you usually get that your home or office is "under fire" from these poison arrows is an accumulation of clutter and unnecessary debris.

Many feng shui cures aimed at deflecting negative energy – such as a tassel, a crystal hanging on some string, or a potted plant – can be placed directly in front of the sharply pointed object that is creating the poison arrow. A "bagua" mirror hung above your front door is also very effective in deflecting negative energy radiating from a light pole sited directly opposite your front door (see page 17).

Negative energy can be created by the stagnation of positive energy. This can easily happen when you have a lot of objects stored around you, or when the room is painted in dark colors, or when it is not illuminated properly. Incorporating feng shui cures that move in a current, such as wind chimes, can change stagnant negative energy into flowing positive energy. The use of color or light can have the same effect.

Finally, negative energy can develop when positive energy is made to run uninterruptedly through long corridors, beams and roads. By being made to move too fast, this energy becomes extremely aggressive – feng shui cures placed along the passageway will slow it down, and placing a wall in its path will stop it.

Many feng shui cures are very flexible, and can be used either to stimulate positive energy or to deflect negative energy. For instance, color can be used both to soothe and to stimulate. Some feng shui cures can be used to boost particular areas of your life if they are placed in the part of your space that corresponds to those areas (see pages 12–13).

Using a cure to maximum effect

A cure can have enormous effects on your life if you use it to improve the flow of energy in a particular part of your house or workplace. In feng shui, it is believed that each section of your home corresponds to one of eight major aspirations of your life. These aspirations are:

* wealth
* acknowledgment
* relationships
* family and health
* creativity and children
* knowledge
* career
* mentors and travel.

In feng shui beliefs, everything is related – there are powerful, corresponding relationships between such things as these aspirations, the elements (see pages 25–27), and the eight main directions of a compass. An easy way of working out what part of your space corresponds to each of the above eight aspirations is to find out how your space is aligned with regard to the main compass directions – north, south, east and west.

Look at your house plan or draw one, and find where north lies. North corresponds to your career aspiration. If you want a career change or improvement in your working conditions, make sure that the northern area of your house is tidy, clean and uncluttered, and include a feng shui cure, such as a melodious-sounding wind chime hanging from the window (see also pages 60–65), to enhance the flow of positive energy in that area.

Relationships correspond to the southwest (see pages 54–59), while health corresponds to the east (see pages 66–71) and education relates to the northeast (see pages 72–77). Here is a table indicating the relationship between the aspirations, the compass directions, and the eight categories of feng shui cures (see pages 6–7).

ASPIRATION	COMPASS DIRECTION	CATEGORY OF FENG SHUI CURES
Wealth	Southeast	Plants and pets
Acknowledgment and fame	South	Reflective objects and lights
Relationships	Southwest	Flutes and fans or mobiles and flags
Family and health	East	Electrical equipment or flutes and fans
Creativity and children	West	Statues and rocks
Knowledge	Northeast	Color or electrical equipment
Career	North	Mobiles and flags or color
Mentors and travel	Northwest	Sound

13

A-Z of Feng Shui Cures

Animal symbols

Incorporating animal motifs in your home or office space is believed to bring the "energy" of that animal into your life (for a discussion of birds and other flying creatures, see page 19). A number of animals are believed to symbolize various beneficial aspects, such as luck, longevity, and prosperity. For example, the proper placement of a fish tank of goldfish attracts luck in financial matters.

In Chinese astrology, it is believed that twelve animals epitomize various forms of destiny and related characteristics, with each animal signifying a particular Chinese year. The rat is the first animal in the twelve-year cycle – it is symbolic of cunning, charisma, and leadership. There is a belief that you can expect prosperity if you unexpectedly find a rat in your home or office.

The table opposite lists the twelve Chinese astrological animals, a range of corresponding years (remember, the Chinese New Year starts at various dates that are always later than the Western New Year), and the animal's symbolic characteristic.

CHINESE ASTROLOGICAL ANIMAL	RANGE OF YEARS	SYMBOLIC CHARACTERISTIC
Rat	1948, 1960, 1972, 1984	Leadership
Ox	1949, 1961, 1973, 1985	Strength
Tiger	1950, 1962, 1974, 1986	Courage
Rabbit	1951, 1963, 1975, 1987	Harmony
Dragon	1952, 1964, 1976, 1988	Power
Snake	1953, 1965, 1977, 1989	Wisdom
Horse	1954, 1966, 1978, 1990	Sophistication
Sheep	1955, 1967, 1979, 1991	Abundance
Monkey	1956, 1968, 1980, 1992	Wiliness
Rooster	1957, 1969, 1981, 1993	Confidence
Dog	1958, 1970, 1982, 1994	Protection
Pig	1959, 1971, 1983, 1995	Honesty

Artwork

In feng shui, harmony and balance are considered to be two of the most important aspects of interior design. Artworks that are placed in a home or office to encourage luck and prosperity are usually harmonious in terms of color and subject matter.

Paintings of pleasant landscapes (and other subjects) that show skill and include flowing lines and harmonious blends of color are a desirable addition to any home and office.

Large paintings are usually placed in hallways and entrances. Large paintings and other artworks, such as statues, must always be placed in areas with a lot of space. This is not only for aesthetic reasons – it also stems from an understanding of the balance between yin (passive) and yang (aggressive) energy in a room. An artwork, particularly if it is large or uses a lot of reds, oranges, and gold, is akin to yang energy, and requires, as balance, a lot more space (yin energy). Always choose a brightly colored piece of artwork for large spaces or to brighten a dark area.

Feng shui practitioners often remove scenes of battles, storms and broken objects to improve morale in a workplace or to help in mending the relationships between family members. Pictures of turbulent water may need to be removed as well – they are thought to have a negative effect on your wealth, making your finances unstable.

Bagua

The bagua is an important image in feng shui. It is an eight-sided flat object, usually with a mirror or the symbol of yin and yang in the middle, and is painted red, green, and gold (mirrors are further discussed on page 37). Between the central image and the edges there are eight trigrams, which symbolize a great many things, such as the eight main compass directions (see pages 12–13), the eight aspirations, the eight cures, and even the eight types of family relationships.

These trigrams also form part of the sixty-four hexagrams used in the I-Ching, or Book of Changes, an ancient Chinese form of divination. The broken lines in the trigrams are symbolic of yin energy, and the unbroken lines represent yang energy.

The bagua is thought to signify the fundamental aspects of life, and as such is used as a powerful symbol of protection. As it is such a potent symbol, it is advisable to use the symbol only on the outside of a building.

It is particularly effective for deflecting poison arrows created by poles, sharply angled rooflines and straight roads. Hang the bagua (with a mirror in the center) above a door or window from where you can see a road, pole or roofline, to deflect the negative energy emanating from these features.

Bells

Bells are extremely useful feng shui cures for reactivating energy in stagnant areas of a building, such as corners and dark rooms. Bells used for feng shui must make a melodious sound when struck.

A room that has a lot of clutter in it, or that is full of large pieces of furniture, can cause stagnant energy. This stagnant energy can give rise to a feeling of blockage in your life. Depending on where the stagnant energy lies, you may experience obstacles in your work, finances or relationships (see pages 12–13). One of the indicators of stagnant energy, apart from the accumulation of clutter, is having arguments or disagreements in that area.

To clear the energy in a stagnant area, simply walk into the space ringing a melodious sounding bell. Stop when you feel that the colors in the room seem clearer or the tone of the bell seems purer.

Bells are also symbolic of peace, and can be hung in the house to attract a better flow of energy. They are especially effective at the end of long corridors, where the energy has had a chance to build up to a fast pace, creating a negative force.

Birds and other creatures that fly

Representations of birds and other creatures that fly are often used as feng shui cures to attract love and harmony. For example, symbols of two ducks or geese represent happiness in marriage or a relationship. Birds and butterflies, especially in pairs, are also symbolic of love. Keep a butterfly carved from jade near you to attract love and romance.

To attract luck into your life, keep a symbol of the bat somewhere near you, such as at the entrance to your bedroom or work space. You may be able to find a feng shui brass bat charm that is decorated with tassels, coins, and small bells. This special "cure" can be hung in the hall near the front entrance to your home, or in the reception area of your office, to deflect negative financial energy and stimulate the flow of positive energy.

In an office, a picture of an eagle flying high above the landscape is an excellent symbol of a manager who is able to see the "big picture;" the head of the company would benefit from a picture of an eagle perched on black rock – this evokes a sense of far-sighted vision and a business approach that is based on strength and experience.

Candles

Candles are symbolic of the element of fire (see page 25), and can be used to best effect in areas such as the fame and acknowledgment space (the south) and the relationship space (the southwest) of your home or room or workplace.

Objects that represent fire should not generally be used in the creativity/children area (the west) or the mentors/travel space (the northwest). Fire is an aggressive yang element that attracts strong, positive energy to strengthen relationships and confidence. This strong energy should not be used in areas that correspond to children, who have a lot of yang energy already, or when seeking to attract powerful friends, as too much yang energy will cause conflict rather than support.

When using candles, always make sure that you use an even number. This is of particular importance in the relationship area. By using two candles in this area, you are attracting an energy that corresponds to the formation of "pairs" or couples (see pages 54–59).

Red candles are often used to stimulate the energy in a particular aspect of your life (see page 22). Black candles symbolize strength; white candles represent purity and peacefulness.

Coins

Chinese coins are often used in feng shui to attract positive energy for financial ventures or to stimulate the flow of wealth and abundance into a home or business. Chinese coins are usually replicas that are dull gold in color; they are round with a square hole. They vary in size and can be found made up into charms that sometimes include other features that signify success and luck, such as a jade bead and a red tassel.

The number of coins used is important. Package three Chinese coins in a pile with red string and place the package on an account book to attract money to your business. Place the package on the top left-hand side of your desk when you are going to ask for a promotion that involves a higher salary. Place the coins in a red envelope and carry this with you when you ask your bank manager for a loan.

You can also obtain a six-coin charm where the coins are secured in a row with a jade bead and red tassel at the end. Hang this from the back of your chair to counter any negative energy that is aimed at you (if your back is facing the entrance to your workplace) or to deflect negative comments from work colleagues.

Color

Strong yang colors such as red, orange, yellow, or gold can be used to stimulate energy in dark areas or in places where clutter seems to habitually accumulate. Red, black, and gold are also often used to stimulate prosperity in a home, shop, or office. Use color to stimulate the energy in the creativity or children area of your home (see pages 12–13).

In feng shui, color is used in harmony with the five elements: earth, water, fire, wood, and metal (see pages 25–27). Over the centuries, Chinese philosophies have determined the correspondences between these elements and various other aspects of life. For instance, the element of earth governs the center of the house, so this is a good area to include yellow, earthy, and golden-hued colors.

Similarly, the element of water governs the northern portion of the house, which may be decorated with blue hues and colors with a touch of black in them. The element of fire rules over the southern part of the house. Decorate this area with reds and oranges. The eastern portion of your home should have some blues and greens in the color scheme to connect it with the element of wood, while the west would benefit from being decorated with whites, creams and silvers, to encourage the energy of the element of metal. To minimize the effect of overhead beams, paint them white (or any light color).

Crystals

Crystals are an excellent tool for clearing negative energy from your space. Man-made crystals, called lead crystal, are those that are faceted and made with a certain percentage of lead. Feng shui practitioners also use semi-precious stones as cures.

Faceted lead crystals are particularly useful for breaking up negative energy – hang these over clutter to help disperse the energy built up there. They will help clear the clutter and keep the area clear of rubbish and unnecessary things. If your property has a large formal interior, consider using lead crystal chandeliers as lighting, particularly if the faceting on each piece is even in number. If you have an unpleasant aspect outside your window, such as a blank wall or an industrial plant, hang the crystal in the window to scatter the negative energy.

Naturally occurring crystals, such as clear quartz crystal, can be placed in the fame and acknowledgment area of your space to stimulate the flow of energy and to enhance your prospects of being noticed (in terms of your career) or being heard (in your family).

Place naturally occurring crystals such as fluorite in the corner of your study to ensure that you are able to focus on your work, and to attract success for your exams and assignments. Use a piece of jade in your relationships area to bring stability to your love life. Citrine is an excellent crystal to attract abundance, and can be used in the wealth area of your home or office.

Curtains

Curtains and other window coverings are very important in feng shui, as it is considered most inauspicious to leave a window exposed so that when night falls the windowpanes grow dark. It is thought that darkness encourages the presence of an undesirable and unbalancing amount of yin or passive energy in the home, which will need to be counterbalanced by other remedies, such as leaving lights on and using yang or bright colors (see page 22) in the area surrounding the window.

Flowing lengths of curtains are considered an auspicious method of covering a window, as they mask the corners of the window, which can create poison arrows that also need to be countered.

Curtains are also useful in screening poison arrows created by outside objects – such as power poles and straight roads that lead to the house – and in covering an undesirable view from the window, which may generate negative energy.

Consider using curtains on your windows if you live near a particularly yang type of place, such as a school, a power station, an industrial area, a railway, or an airport, using the fabric to screen you from the strong, aggressive energy created by the movement of a lot of people.

Similarly, use curtains if you live near a particularly yin type of place where there is a build-up of stagnant energy, such as a garbage dump, sewage outlet, a church, or a place of mourning.

Elements
(Earth, Fire, Metal,
Water, Wood)

Feng shui, Eastern philosophies, and medicine recognize five elements: earth, fire, metal, water, and wood. It is believed that these elements, in various permutations, make up everything in our world, including ourselves.

Each element "rules" the type of energy that flows in a particular part of the house. For instance, the earth is considered to govern the center of the house, while water is related to the north, fire to the south, wood to the east and metal to the west.

To encourage the flow of this elemental energy in your space and life, place an item that corresponds to the energy of the element at each wall, facing the appropriate compass direction or in the center of a room.

ELEMENT	DIRECTION	ORNAMENTS CORRESPONDING TO THE ELEMENT
Earth	Center	Stoneware and other ceramics made of earthy colors, and potted plants
Fire	South	Candles, heaters, or fireplaces
Metal	West	Silver or white statues or wind chimes
Water	North	A small water feature or a fish tank
Wood	East	Potted plants and wooden-framed mirrors or pictures

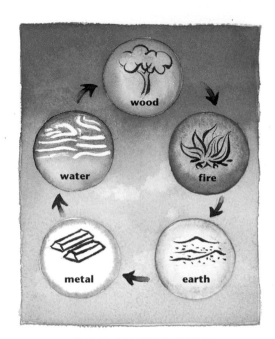

THE PRODUCTIVE CYCLE

The flow of elemental energy can be further enhanced by including an object representing another element that feng shui practitioners believe will support and strengthen the power of the original element. For instance, if we want to strengthen the element of fire and the corresponding sense of creativity and forceful energy, we could add a wooden candlestick to the candle in the south of our space. The illustrations above and opposite depict the flow of both creative and destructive elemental energies in feng shui.

Many energy problems in a home or office occur because there is a destructive relationship between the elements. Feng shui practitioners over the centuries have used their knowledge of the flow of creative and destructive energies to help them work out why certain problems keep occurring in a person's home or life, and to suggest simple but effective solutions.

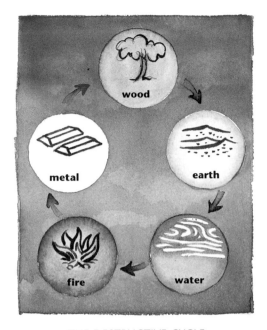

THE DESTRUCTIVE CYCLE

The destructive cycle is merely an indication that when one element, such as fire, is put together with an element that is destructive, such as water, the element of fire will not be strengthened, but will transmute into another substance, such as steam. Fire itself is detrimental to metal, because fire causes metal to lose its integrity and metamorphose into something else.

The illustration above also gives you a solution if your home has some tense energy created by a destructive relationship between elements, such as if you have a metal statue standing next to a potted plant. Either move the statue or plant away from each other or place a water feature between them to break the disruptive flow of energy.

Fish tanks

Watching fish swimming in a fish tank is relaxing, and, depending on the fish you have chosen and the shape of the tank, may attract abundance and wealth into your home or business.

The best position for the fish tank is in the southeast, the area corresponding to the wealth aspect of your space. Always include some greenery in your fish tank, choosing only those plants that will help your fish to thrive.

Choose red goldfish for your fish tank. The number of fish also affects the flow of energy. You should have any even number of goldfish except four, although four is a number usually associated with the southeast. In China, four is the number closely associated with death – the way of pronouncing the two words is very similar.

Another belief, one of the few exceptions to the even number rule, is that you should have nine fish in your fish tank – eight goldfish and one black fish. The number eight is auspicious for good business and wealth, while the black fish has the role of "eating" all the negative energy around you.

Floor rugs

Floor rugs are useful and relatively easy ways of introducing color into an interior to balance yin and yang energy. If the space is large and the furniture is positioned around the wall, you may want to find a rug for the middle of the floor, using mainly yang colors, such as reds, oranges, and yellows. If the rug is placed in the center of the room, it is best to have some earthy colors in its design, because the middle of the room, as well as the middle of the house, corresponds to the element of earth.

Rugs correspond to the element of earth because, for example, they are made from fibres that come from creatures that graze on the fruits of the earth. Accordingly, they are also best placed in a central hallway or in the western areas of the building, which correspond to the element of metal.

For most residential interiors, it would be auspicious to choose rugs that have a harmonious blend of colors – a solid block of strong color may unbalance the flow of yin and yang energies within the house.

Auspicious rug designs can include lines of black, which not only give the design strength and definition but also symbolize success and confidence. The designs should be fluid and rounded rather than angular and geometric. However, the shape of the bagua (see page 17), which is based on the octagon, is still considered auspicious, especially if there is a circular motif in its center. Circular or oval rugs will help to stimulate the flow of energy in a room.

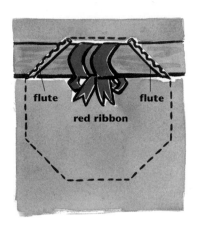

Flutes

Flutes are particularly useful in deflecting the fast, hitting energy caused by overhead beams. The negative energy effects of exposed overhead beams must be minimized – they are believed to cause innumerable problems in health and emotional stability.

It is considered inauspicious to sit under a beam, as it may cause headaches and migraines. Similarly, if you sleep under a beam, health problems will occur wherever the beam crosses your body. For example, if you suffer from ulcers, check that you are not sleeping under an overhead beam that crosses your stomach.

Flutes made of bamboo are often used by feng shui practitioners, and are linked with the element of wood. They can be used to deflect a poison arrow created by wooden elements in the house such as columns or straight corridors.

Pairs of bamboo flutes are often used to break the rapid energy flow created by straight lines. They should be placed at a forty-five degree angle to the beam, cornice or architrave. If they are placed parallel to the flow of energy, they will slow it down only minimally. It is best to position the flutes with their mouthpieces facing downward, and to make sure that they are angled toward each other.

Fruit

Fruit, in many cultures, is a symbol of wealth and prosperity. Likewise, in feng shui, fruit is often placed in high places in a living or dining room to signify abundance. Yang-colored fruits, such as red pomegranates, oranges, and pineapples, are particularly used. Fruits that are ripe and well rounded are considered auspicious.

To attract abundance to your home, place the ripe or ripening fruit in a gold-colored (for wealth) or red (for success) bowl. Then place the bowl on a high shelf in the dining, living, or family room. The abundance will be doubled if you place the bowl somewhere where it and the fruit are reflected in a mirror – on the mantelpiece or the sideboard/buffet, for example.

If you are using this cure, be vigilant about changing the display whenever the fruit becomes tired or starts to rot. Otherwise, consider using good-quality plastic fruit or, even better, painted wooden fruit, making sure to keep the display clean.

Fruit trees can also be planted in a suitable spot in the garden to attract abundance to the family or business. A fruit tree on either side of an entrance facing southeast would assure that a prosperous energy enters the house. A peach tree is often planted to encourage success in marriage.

Furniture

Western furniture is usually an assembly of squares and rectangles rather than fluid, rounded shapes and carving, which would better suit many feng shui principles. However, there are many ways we can incorporate feng shui concepts and minimize some of the poison arrows caused by the edges of furniture.

Upholster chairs and stools with soft, comfortable fabric in fluid, harmonious designs. Seat cushions can be tied on to soften the lines of a hardback chair. Scatter cushions will also help stimulate the energy of seating furniture (see page 42).

Square and rectangular tables are notorious for creating poison arrows of energy. When choosing a table, feng shui practitioners would recommend a circular or oval table with space for an even number of chairs. However, do not despair if you have a square or rectangular table – consider some of the following suggestions.

* Keep a tablecloth, preferably printed with a fluid pattern, on the table at all times.
* Use round or oval place mats at meal times to minimize the outbreak of arguments and disagreements (these can be aggravated by sharply angled pieces of furniture).
* Place a circular glass bowl, filled with water and perhaps a couple of floating candles (always an even number) and some flowers or pretty leaves, on the table (make sure the bowl is in proportion to the table).

The shelves of open bookcases also cause poison arrows, so it's worth reconsidering the need for bookshelves in your home or office. If you do need them, never have them positioned so that the poison arrows they create are aimed at your back or your head. If you sit with your back to a bookcase, you may find that you suffer from back pain or that you suffer through backstabbing colleagues. If you sit facing a bookshelf or have a hutch over your desk or study area, you may suffer from headaches and eyestrain. Another solution is to add glass doors to an open bookcase – this will help screen the flow of poison arrows.

When choosing your furniture, consider the proportions of the furniture and be especially careful that the item is not too big for the room, creating yang energy that will need to be balanced with a yin-colored floor rug nearby. Proportions and measurements are very important. For particularly expensive or regularly used pieces of furniture, get a feng shui ruler to work out whether your desk, table or other item is auspicious in size.

Feng shui tip

You can make your own feng shui ruler. Get a long piece of tape,
at least 9 feet (3 m), and mark off every 17 inches (432 mm).
Then subdivide each of these sections into eight segments, each measuring
approximately 2 1/8 inch (54 mm). Each of these segments is
identified as auspicious or inauspicious:

* the first segment is auspicious
* the second segment is inauspicious
* the third segment is inauspicious
* the fourth segment is auspicious
* the fifth segment is auspicious
* the sixth segment is inauspicious
* the seventh segment is inauspicious
* the eighth segment is auspicious.

Hedges

Hedges are used extensively in feng shui to deflect the negative energy created by poison arrows and to filter positive energy through to your front door. Use hedges to protect and to help direct positive energy up to your front door or reception area – these are the main entrances through which energy enters your home or office. Hedges are effective protection if your home or workplace is positioned with a road leading up to the front door. You can also use hedges to shield any windows through which you can see a road, a pole, or an angled roof aimed straight at you.

Many different types of shrubs can be successfully turned into hedges. Those that have, in certain seasons, a scent, bright flowers, or brightly colored leaves are favored in feng shui gardening, as these attract positive energy, and this energy will flow from your garden into your home.

Avoid creating clipped, hard-edged hedges, especially if you are growing a box hedge. Prune your hedge into a formal rounded shape or plan an informal hedge instead. Also consider including in your hedge a round-leafed plant such as the firethorn (*Pyracantha* species).

A few ideas for high hedges

Scented hedges – orange jessamine (*Murraya paniculata*)
Brightly flowered hedges – camellias (such as *Camellia sasanqua*)
Hedges with brightly colored leaves – photinia (such as *Photinia* 'Rubens')

Insects

The category of insects includes butterflies and cicadas. These insects are often incorporated into Chinese art, as part of the flowing landscape scenes depicted on screens, wall hangings, and beautifully translucent porcelain bowls and dishes.

Symbols of these creatures can be used in an interior to invoke a certain type of energy. Many of these insect symbols can also be found carved in various semiprecious stones, such as green jade.

The butterfly is a symbol of joy and attracts positive energy into the house. Place an unframed picture of a butterfly where there is a lot of space, to encourage a more carefree feeling to enter your life. It is important not to have the butterfly image closely surrounded by other objects, as its energy dissipates quickly if stifled.

The cicada is a symbol of joy, as well as having the mythic quality of being able to promote immortality. A cicada carved in jade, a stone which is often used for symbols related to health, is used by some feng shui practitioners to counter illness in the house.

Lamps and lighting

The position of table and floor lamps can work very effectively to stimulate stagnant energy in a house or workplace – lamps are often used in the southern part of the building to stimulate the acknowledgment and fame area of your life.

Light that floods downward helps energy to flow around the house or workplace. Rounded lamp bases are desirable – light will bounce off an angular lamp base and create a movement of negative energy. Use floor lamps that angle light upward to stimulate dark corners, dark-colored rooms and rooms that do not get much sunlight. These floor lamps will also help alleviate feelings of depression. Balance is important in feng shui, so make sure you place lamps in pairs where possible.

Outside lighting is an important way of deflecting poison arrows aimed at your front door. Use a low-wattage light bulb, and leave the outside light on or leave the entrance hall light on permanently.

If your front door is below street level, install a light fitting that spreads light upward. This will give the impression that your front door is higher up than it really is.

Mirrors

Mirrors are exceptionally useful feng shui tools, especially for manipulating the flow of energy in the house. Flat mirrors can be used to stimulate energy in the fame and acknowledgment area. However, if your fame and acknowledgment area is in your bedroom, do not place a mirror there. It is considered most unlucky to have a mirror in the bedroom.

Mirrors can also be placed to reflect a pleasant view from outside – this is a cheap way to bring more of the garden or nature into the building. It may also be a useful way of enhancing the wealth sector (the southeastern section) of your building, as the wood in a frame is excellent for attracting abundance and prosperity. In feng shui, a mirror positioned symmetrically on each of two walls that meet as a protruding corner can effectively negate the poison arrow that would normally be created by that corner.

Mirrors can also be used to "mask" an entire area. For example, if your bathroom and toilet are not auspiciously placed – if they are positioned in the wealth sector of the house or can be seen from the front door – you can place a mirror on the toilet or bathroom door to "hide" the room from sight. Feng shui practitioners also like to use mirrors that are convex. These mirrors deflect negative energy by distorting the image – and thus dispersing the energy – rather than simply reflecting the image. These mirrors are often incorporated into a bagua (see page 17).

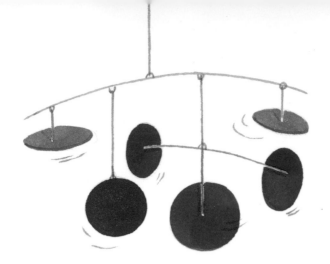

Mobiles

The word "feng" in feng shui refers to the force of the wind, which is how beneficial energy moves. Mobiles, flags, and other objects that are made to move with the wind attract beneficial energy as well as dispersing any poison arrows.

These cures can be used in the north part of your home to stimulate your career, or in the southwest to add a bit more fun and light-heartedness to your relationship, especially if you and your partner have been experiencing very strong emotions (either positive or negative).

If you are sitting or sleeping under a beam, consider placing a banner or flags along the beam. If you sit under a beam and cannot move your chair or desk elsewhere, hang a mobile immediately above your head. This will help disperse any negative energy that was descending upon you and possibly causing you headaches, stress, or feelings of anger.

Mobiles should be placed where they will move slightly in the breeze, such as in front of a ventilation grille or outside on a sheltered balcony. If your mobile falls down in the breeze, consider using another cure in that area – perhaps hang a crystal on the inside of a nearby window.

Pets

Like plants, having pets around the house is an excellent way to stimulate energy in your space. Pets as feng shui cures are best used to improve the flow of energy in your finances. You may position their bed or feeding bowl so that the animal or animals will go through the wealth sector (in the southeastern part of your house) to reach them. For comments about fish, see page 28.

It is auspicious to have two pets, preferably one female (yin) and one male (yang), and to allow them to play at random throughout the house (after some suitable house training!), as animals have a natural tendency to flow with the energy and focus on troublesome spots. Watch the movement of your older animals to see which areas they like and which they avoid – this will be a good indication of energy problems.

Young cats, in particular, appear to thrive on helping you clear your clutter by, for instance, disturbing mounds of accumulated material.

Getting young animals is also a great encouragement to clear the house of clutter. However, if their energy becomes too yang (overly stimulated), consider giving them a dark blue collar or coat to help balance their high spirits with yin (passive) energy – or, better still, take them for a walk or let them go outside for a short period of time.

Feng shui tip

Place two small statues of little cats called "Lucky Cats" on a cash register or in the wealth segment of your desk (the top left-hand side) to attract financial abundance.

Plants

Indoor plants stimulate the flow of abundance to your home or business if they can congregate near the southeastern area of your space, which corresponds to your wealth aspiration. Plants that have rounded leaves and prominent woody stems are particularly auspicious in this area.

Some of the most auspicious plants include the prosperity bamboo (*Canifolia*), the Chinese money tree (*Portulacaria afra*), the dracaena (of which there are many varieties), and the cumquat (*Fortunella*). To further enhance the prosperity of these plants, insert a gold-colored feng shui coin into the soil.

To stimulate the energy in the central part of the building, an area that corresponds to the element of earth, use leafy plants. Make sure the plants in this area receive enough attention and light, as a dying plant not only indicates the presence of stagnant energy but will also contribute to a feeling of sluggishness in the area, which could affect the health of the family or the finances of the business.

Another auspicious position for an indoor plant – some bamboo kept in a pot is good for this – is just inside the front door or along a corridor leading off the entrance hall, particularly if the back door can be seen from the front door. Having the front and back doors aligned so that the energy shoots straight through the house without having the opportunity to meander and curve its beneficial energy around leads to negative energy – this can be alleviated by placing a plant in a position that will deflect the energy from its straight course. Fragrant indoor plants, such as herbs grown near a window, will also encourage the flow of energy through the house.

Plants can be used to deflect other architectural poison arrows, such as those created by columns and protruding corners, by being placed in front of the column or corners. Plants can also be used to soften the rectangular outlines of some of the larger pieces of furniture in your space, by being placed by the corner. Small and colorful potted plants, such as African violets (*Saintpaulia*), can also grace the center of your rectangular or square table to alleviate the flow of negative energy around your family and guests at meal times.

Having the back of the building "protected" by mountains is considered especially auspicious. These "mountains" can be in the form of a wooded area, or a large structure such as a bathhouse. If you do not have such "mountains," consider putting some plants in big earthenware pots at the back of your property to stabilize supportive energy in your life and work.

See also Hedges on page 34 and Water features on page 46.

Scatter cushions

Scatter cushions are a cheap and effective way of introducing differently colored fabrics to a room to balance the flow of energy in terms of yin and yang (see page 22) and the elements (see pages 25–27).

Colors such as gold, red, and black are particularly good feng shui colors to introduce into an interior as they symbolize wealth, good fortune, success, and strength. However, in most modern Western interiors these colors can only be used as accents, not as a base.

The softness of scatter cushions is also important. This softness represents yin (female) energy, and is an excellent way to balance hard surfaces, such as sofas, chairs, and long low coffee tables, which are symbolic of yang (male) energy.

Always remember to have an even number of scatter cushions and to make sure that they are attractively displayed so that they do not give an impression of clutter.

Screens

Screens are an effective way to mask undesirable or inauspiciously positioned rooms, such as a toilet that can be seen from the front door or from a person's office. Also, place a screen in front of a door that leads to the toilet or bathroom if your dinner guests can see the toilet bowl or basin through the open door when they are seated at the table.

In feng shui, it is believed to be unlucky to sit with your back to the entrance to your office, study or bedroom. In a conference situation, or if you are working in an open plan office, you may wish to place a moveable screen across the entrance, or put a pot plant there, to protect your back.

As screens usually have a strong rectangular appearance, which can create poison arrows through the space, you should soften the screen's lines – either drape fabric over the panels, or choose a screen where the uprights holding the panel are unobtrusive or lightly colored, or a screen where the fabric is completely wrapped around the frame. Chinese screens always have images of pleasant rural landscapes, enhanced by a fluid design and harmonious colors.

If the toilet is particularly inauspiciously placed, such as on the floor immediately above the front door or reception area, you may also wish to

hang tassels from each panel of the screen that you place in front of the toilet – this will disperse the negative, stagnant energy created by the position of the room.

Sounds

The sound of melodious music is a powerful way to stimulate positive energy and help it flow through the house. Use music to clear negative, stagnant energy, particularly from the northwestern segment of the building, which corresponds to mentors and travel, or in the northeastern area, which relates to the knowledge aspiration.

Your sound system, television, or radio can be set up in these areas of the building to stimulate these aspects of your life. Ringing bells (see page 18) and using wind chimes (see page 47) are other, more traditional ways of using sound as a feng shui cure. Sound is also an excellent cure to use in an overly dark, shaded, yin room.

However, be wary about electrical sounds, such as the constant low-pitched whirring produced by machines that are switched on. Feng shui practitioners frown on keeping an electric clock near the bedside table and on having a television or stereo in the bedroom. The sounds these appliances make (even when they are not "on") are believed to interfere with your rest because they constantly stimulate the energy in a room.

Televisions and stereos generate yang energy, so they are best kept in a cabinet or covered with a yin-colored cloth – this will rebalance their energy. If you are constantly at work in front of a computer screen, the sound of water will help revitalize you.

Statues

Statues and other heavy objects are useful for slowing down fast-moving energy. They can be placed at the head or the base of a straight staircase, or at the front door, or at the door leading into the reception area (if there is a straight path leading from the street to the front door or reception area). They will help positive energy enter the building at a more graceful pace. They are also used to stabilize the energy in the west of the building, which corresponds to the children/creativity aspiration.

Statues should be of a size proportionate to their surroundings. Overly large statues in small areas or rooms will unbalance the energy in those spaces. It is also important that the statues are generally rounded, and do not have any protruding sharp edges that may create poison arrows.

Avoid Western statues that show a person or animal in distress or in anger – this may cause negative energy to circulate, stultifying the energy in the surrounding area. Use statues and sculptures that give a sense of peace, balance, and harmony.

The statue of the Lord Buddha is becoming increasingly popular in the West. It can be placed in the interior to evoke harmony. Another popular variant is the statue of a fat, happy Buddha, usually called the "Laughing Buddha," which can be placed in the garden, facing the building, to attract abundance to the family or business.

Water features

Water features such as indoor water fountains, fish tanks (see page 28), outdoor ponds, and birdbaths are often placed in a space to promote a sense of abundance in a person's home and business.

Water features also useful in dispersing the negative energy of poison arrows created by poles and other sharp-angled features of the environment outside your building. A business situated at a T-intersection was able to stop the force of the poison arrow aimed at its reception area by placing an attractively landscaped pool in front of the reception area.

Pools should be slightly curved or kidney shaped rather than straight edged, and the curves should appear to "hug" the building. It is important to keep the water moving – it should not be allowed to become stagnant.

Some feng shui practitioners believe that water features, including fish tanks, should not be placed on the left-hand side (looking from the inside) of the interior of a building, as this will bring bad luck to the female occupants. The reason for this is that water is a yin type of element and when placed on the yin (or left) side of the building, it can unbalance the female energy in the space.

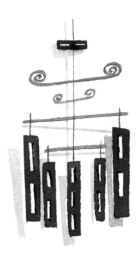

Wind chimes

Melodious-sounding wind chimes are often used to slow down energy that is moving too fast down a garden path or a corridor or along a beam. If you sit under a beam, either move or hang a wind chime directly overhead to dissipate the negative, oppressive energy that the beam is directing down toward you. Also, consider hanging a wind chime in front of a protruding corner to dissipate the poison arrows created in that area.

Wind chimes are often positioned in an entrance hall to encourage the beneficial energy to move with curvaceous grace through the rest of the house – they are excellent for distributing energy. For the interior of a building, use only hollow metal or bamboo wind chimes, preferably with five or six tubes.

Wind chimes can also be used to stimulate and improve the flow of energy in the northwest section of the building, which corresponds to the mentors and travel aspiration.

Solid metal wind chimes can be hung outside your front door to attract positive energy to you, especially if your front door faces west or north. Do not use this cure if your entrance faces east – this compass direction corresponds to the element of wood, which is capable of being "destroyed" by metal.

Using Feng Shui Cures
MONEY

Attracting wealth and prosperity

Many feng shui cures are tailor-made to attract wealth and prosperity to a home or business. There are two main areas that require attention to attract a sense of abundance: the entrance and the southeastern section of the building, which corresponds to wealth and abundance. In each of these areas, go through the feng shui cure preparation checklist on the opposite page to first "cleanse" the space. Now you are ready to use one of the following feng shui objects in each area to attract abundance to you. To attract an abundant energy through your front door, do one of the following:

* hang a bagua (see page 17) outside and above the front door;
* place a "laughing Buddha" (see page 47) in the garden so that he is facing the front door;
* place a "lucky frog" either facing the front door or just inside the front door, facing in; or
* hang a set of solid metal rod wind chimes (see page 47) outside and above your front door.

To stimulate abundance in the southeastern section of the building, do one of the following things:

* install a fish tank with healthy goldfish (see page 28);
* place a woody-stemmed pot plant in the area (see page 40–41); or
* hang a prosperity charm (made up of a variety of prosperous items, such as symbols of fish, coins, small bells, jade balls, and red tassels) in the largest window in the area.

ACTION PLAN FOR EACH AREA	SUITABLE FENG SHUI CURE
Check for poison arrows: if you see, through a window, a poison arrow caused by an external feature, remove or disguise the cause of the poison arrow	EXTERNAL SOLUTION – Plant a hedge (see page 34) or position a pond or other water feature between your building and the object causing the poison arrow (see page 46). INTERNAL SOLUTION – Install curtains (see page 24); hang a crystal in the window (see page 23); put a pair of small brass lions in the window facing the direction from which the poison arrow is being created; or hang a mobile (see page 38), a banner of flags or tassels, or wind chimes (see page 47) from the window.
Remove clutter to allow energy to flow unimpeded through each area	Hang a clear quartz crystal (see page 23) or a melodious-sounding wind chime (see page 47) over the clutter, or keep the light on in the area until the clutter is cleared (see page 36).
Check each corner in the area	If the area feels stagnant (dust is collecting in the corners, and the colors appear muted), clap your hands or ring a bell (see page 18) in each corner. If the corner protrudes into the room, hang a crystal (see page 23) or wind chime (see page 47) from the ceiling; place a mirror on each wall (see page 37); or place a plant (see page 40–41) or a silk flower arrangement in front of the corner's edge.
Remove or cover objects that create negative energy in this area	Remove large metal objects from the southeastern section of the house.

Keeping hold of money

If you feel that no matter how much money you bring into the home or the business, you still never seem to have enough, then you may need to find out if your money energy is flowing out of the house unchecked. In feng shui beliefs, water is always linked with money. If there is a steady water leak somewhere in the building, there will be a subsequent drain on your financial resources.

When you have the feeling that money is slipping through your fingers, check the following:

* is your toilet, bath, sink or other drain situated in the southeastern section of your building?
* is the plumbing in the building maintained properly?

If the southeastern section of your building contains a toilet, bathroom, kitchen, or sink, do one of the following to "cure" the situation and restore a flow of abundance to you and your business:

* keep the toilet lid down when flushing so that you are "disguising" the drainage of water/money from your building;
* place a mirror (see page 37) on the toilet seat or on your toilet and bathroom doors, or place a screen (see page 43) in front of

the door leading to the room with the toilet or basin, again "hiding" the room symbolically and indicating that the room does not exist;

* keep the plugs in sink and basin drains and cover the grilles of floor drains with cotton rugs that still "breathe," or with raised wooden slat platforms; or

* tie red threads to as many golden feng shui coins (see page 21) as you have drain holes and hang a coin over each drain hole, from the ceiling, tap or shelf above the sink.

If you have found that one of your drains is leaking and the plumber is delayed, consider hanging a special coin charm over the offending pipe or over the drain outlet. This feng shui cure is a six-coin charm – a row of overlapping coins threaded together in a straight line with red thread, ending in a tassel.

Also, see if you have any water features placed near a source of fire, such as a heater, a fireplace or stove. The combination of the fire element and the water element is considered destructive (see pages 26–27). Although water is able to quench fire, heat can also evaporate water over a period of time, and, because of this, it is believed that the combination of water and fire will mean your money will slowly disappear.

If you have a sink or dishwasher next to your stove, place a piece of wood, such as a chopping board, between them, indicating that you are breaking the destructive cycle of fire and water.

Encouraging success in business

To encourage success in business, focus on your areas of business – particularly where you personally work. Look around your office or workplace and follow the feng shui cure preparation checklist on page 49 to cleanse the space before introducing your specially selected feng shui cures.

Once you have cleared the space, focus on removing certain objects that may be attracting bad luck to you without you realizing it. Focus on the pictures near you at work – are they harmonious and attractive? Remove any pictures where the subject matter includes turbulent water, as water and money are closely connected in feng shui, and do not have any battle scenes in your office decor.

Avoid placing pictures of mountains directly in front of where you work or directly in front of the entrance to your work or business space. They will create an obstructive energy that will lead you to encounter one obstacle after another in your business. Place a picture of mountains at your back – this will encourage feelings of strength and support, and is an especially effective cure if you suffer from lower back problems at work.

Pictures that encourage success in your workplace include photographs or images in any media of animals that in feng shui are related to abundance, such as fish, a pheasant, phoenix, boar, or toad (see page 14).

Special money charms featuring frogs are very effective for encouraging a flow of abundance to you. The feng shui "Fortune Frog" can be placed just inside your office door, looking into your workplace. Place him on a shelf rather than on the floor. The "Fortune Frog" is either three-legged or sits on a pile of gold coins. He is usually gold in color and has a slit in his mouth into which you can insert a coin.

If you use files in your work, keep a small cure of three feng shui coins (see page 21) tied into a package with red thread over a file that represents an important project. You can also place this simple package over any documentation or books of accounts that represent the financial status of your business. If you work with a cash register, place the package on top of the machine and place a mirror beside it to multiply the money coming to you. Placing a bell over the register will also stimulate abundant energy.

If you sit at a desk, you can make the tabletop a miniature version of your workplace – the wealth section will correspond to the top left-hand section of your desk. Place one (and only one) of the following feng shui cures in this area to stimulate good business:

* the Fortune Frog;
* a crystal ball made from citrine, a stone that resonates with abundance;
* a special eight-coin charm;
* a jade tree; or
* a flowering pot plant with red or pink flowers, such as an African violet.

RELATIONSHIPS

Attracting romance

Feng shui principles can be successfully applied to attracting the energies of romance and love. Focus on the southwestern area of your home and your bedroom. Follow the feng shui cure preparation checklist on page 49 to clear these two main areas of poison arrows, clutter, and stagnant energy.

Once you have followed the checklist, focus on removing objects that resonate with wood, such as large, heavy timber furniture. Only remove plants from this area if they have a prominent stem. If they are leafy and their foliage is lush, leave them in this area – these plants will enhance the element of earth.

There are other feng shui rules about the placement or removal of objects in the bedroom that relate to your love life. Mirrors, for instance, are thought to be very powerful, magical objects that can create or symbolize a strong flow of yin energy. It is believed to be particularly unlucky for romance if there is a mirror in the bedroom, or if we can see ourselves reflected in a mirror while we are in bed; this is also thought to cause disturbed sleep. The introduction of a mirror in the bedroom shared by a couple symbolizes the introduction of a third person into the relationship.

One powerful feng shui cure to attract happiness and fidelity in a marriage is placing two duck figurines onto a small, round mirror that comfortably accommodates them – in this case the mirror symbolizes peaceful, calm waters. Pictures of a pair of cranes or geese could be used instead, as both these creatures symbolize fidelity in marriage.

Another thing to watch and "cure" is the presence of a beam over the bed. You may have troubles in your relationship if the beam runs above the bed in such a way that you sleep on one side and your partner sleeps on the other. However, arguments may be minimized (see pages 56–57) if you use a simple feng shui cure – a red ribbon tied across the beam, a banner of flags tied along the length of the beam (at least that part that hits the bed), two flutes (see page 30), or some wind chimes (see page 47).

If you wish to attract a new relationship, here are a number of feng shui cures that can be placed in the southwestern part of your home or in your bedroom. These will generate an energy that will stimulate the flow of love and romance to you:

* a picture of a pair of birds (see page 19) or butterflies (see page 35);
* a floor lamp that is left switched on (see also page 36);
* a yang-colored (reds, oranges, and pinks) fan or a pair of flutes with red tassels hanging from one end.

Minimizing arguments

Arguments usually occur where the energy flow of your home or office is disturbed, or attacked by a poison arrow, or stagnant. Arguments expend yang energy and can occur as a result of too much of this energy accumulating in one area, either because of a poison arrow or too many pieces of furniture cluttering the area.

When arguments flare up in your home or office, keep a mental note of where they occur and whether you can see any feature in that area that may create a build-up of negative energy or a stagnation of energy. Follow the feng shui cure preparation checklist on page 49 to clear the area first. Also, look up and check whether arguments are occurring under an exposed beam. If they are, try some of the feng shui cures mentioned on pages 54–55.

If a particular person appears to be generating a number of the arguments, also check that there are no poison arrows or negative energy flowing where that person habitually sits, works, or (if appropriate) sleeps. If the person is a member of staff, ensure that they sit or work facing the entrance to their workspace. By constantly having their backs to the entrance, they will continually feel undermined and unappreciated.

Energy that runs fast along a corridor negatively affects not only the corridor but also area where the energy hits, usually a wall that is positioned perpendicular to the corridor. This energy also negatively affects the room or area on the other side of the wall. Note whether the argumentative person has a room – an office or a bedroom – at the end of a corridor. If possible, place some protective shields in this area, otherwise that person will literally feel constantly under attack. At the wall where the energy hits, place a lush, healthy-looking plant to disperse the residual negative energy that is leaking into the room, or hang a picture of an eagle as a protection against bad luck.

If the problem you are suffering is family disruptions, a picture or other image of an animal that symbolizes peace and harmony, such as a rabbit or phoenix, is a good feng shui cure. These animals have yin qualities that will help calm the overstimulation that an excess of yang energy can bring. Place the picture or image in the living room if you are having arguments within the family group, or in the room of the person who appears to have an excess of yang energy.

If this person is a child, you may consider hanging a bell on their door to encourage more peaceful communication between you – the bell helps clear stagnant energy from the child's relationship between itself and the outside world. Also consider giving them a present of a piece of jade (to encourage a sense of stability) or some onyx (for balancing and regulating the emotions).

Once an argument has erupted, clear the energy of the space by clapping your hands or ringing a bell (see page 18) in the corners, using sound as a feng shui cure (see also page 44).

Forging strong friendships

To encourage the flow of friendship and help from powerful people, focus on the northwestern area of your home or office. This area resonates best with feng shui cures that use melodious sounds. First, prepare this area by following the feng shui cure preparation checklist on page 49.

If you are seeking useful friends, such as a person in authority who can help you with your career or studies, in an office or school environment, also focus on the area of your desk that corresponds to the mentors aspiration – the right-hand side of your desk by your right elbow. Place your phone in this area to encourage calls from people who are motivated to help you.

The sound of the phone ringing will also stimulate the flow of beneficial energy toward strong friendships, becoming a useful feng shui cure in itself. However, make sure that the ring of the phone is, if not melodious, at least not strident.

You should remove the phone from this area if you are constantly getting calls. Constant use may cause an overstimulation of energy – this should be avoided. Instead, consider using your cell phone as a feng shui cure, keeping it on the right-hand side of the desk, either on top of the desk or in an uncluttered top right-hand drawer. If possible, program your cell phone to have a simple, pleasant melody as its ringing tone.

As sound is an effective stimulant for this aspiration, hang a six-bar wind chime (see page 47) in the northwestern section of your home or office.

To attract strong friendships and powerful supporters to your family or business, you should hang a bagua (see page 17) over the entrance to your home or office.

Also, focus on your living or family room or staff common room. Follow the preparation checklist on page 49 for the northwestern section of this room and then position a floor lamp in this area (see page 36), leaving the lamp switched on for at least a couple of hours a day.

To encourage compassion and kindness in friends and mentors, place a picture or statue of the powerful Chinese goddess Kuan Yin on a high shelf overlooking the room, preferably where the floor light can highlight the image. Kuan Yin, who is becoming very popular, is the goddess of compassion, and is often depicted holding a lotus flower.

WORK

Getting a new job

When you are looking for new employment or a new career path, it is always wise to clear the energy in your home and office so that you can make way for new opportunities and ideas. Follow the feng shui cure preparation checklist on page 49. Also work out whether or not your worktable or desk is auspicious in measures (see pages 32–33), and make sure you are not sitting too low in relation to your desk (see pages 62–63).

One of the most common problems in a job interview situation is being seated where your back is facing the entrance to the interview room. When you are placed in this position, you are more likely to feel nervous and unable to project yourself in the best possible light. Try to move the chair so that you are facing the doorway and are not so vulnerable. If this is impracticable, don't worry, as there is a way to unobtrusively shield yourself from the energy hitting your back.

Take a black bag or briefcase into the interview room. In feng shui, black symbolizes strength and determination. If you are unable to reposition the chair, simply place the bag behind the chair, as if you are putting it out of the way (after you have taken out the files or other documentation you might need during the interview, of course).

Have a gold feng shui coin nestling near your documentation to encourage success in your interview. Some feng shui practitioners believe that, to strengthen determination and success, you should also take a small gold-colored statue of a goat to your interview.

Before going to the interview, prepare your bag – it should be free from dirt, rubbish, or clutter, and it should have three tassels hanging inside it. Choose a black tassel for a feeling of confidence, a yellow tassel to symbolize your wish to advance in your career, and a purple tassel to help you attract the best remuneration possible.

If you want some extra help, keep the tassels in a compartment where you have also placed a small pocket torch. Keep the torch on during the interview if you know that the light won't show through the bag's zipper or joins and if you won't need to get any documents out of your bag. Otherwise, simply place the torch with the tassels, as a symbol of lighting the path to your goals, which are represented by the tassels.

Succeeding at work

In feng shui, your career resonates with the northern section of your home and office. If you wish to succeed, and to impress your boss or supervisor with your work, install bright cheerful curtains (see page 24) or place scatter cushions (see page 42) made from yang-colored fabrics (see page 22) in your work area.

Your work can be overlooked if you are sitting with your back facing the entrance to your workspace. Try to reposition yourself so that you are facing your entrance, or place a mirror on your desk so that you can see the entrance while you work facing away from the door.

However, if your career feels overstimulated – if your jobs are scattered and you feel you are unfocused and trying to do a hundred things at once – you may wish to rebalance the energy in this area with yin (dark-colored) fabrics or a piece of dark furniture.

This northerly section resonates with the element of water, so remove any large objects that resonate with the element of earth (see pages 25–27), such as large earthenware pots and leafy pot plants. It is very important to keep this area as free from clutter as possible.

Also, remove any dried flowers from this section of both your home and your office, and be vigilant about removing fresh flowers once they start to lose their first flush of beauty and energy. Pictures of mountains that you can see as you are sitting at your desk should be repositioned to hang on the wall behind you.

Follow the feng shui cure preparation checklist on page 49 for both the northerly section of your home and your portion of the workplace, to clear the areas of clutter and deal with any poison arrows. Once you have cleared the spaces, include a picture of a confident creature, such as a monkey or rooster, or place a yellow tassel on your desk to attract promotion. The image of a pagoda is also believed to signify success in business – it symbolizes your ability to rise through the hierarchies at work. Place this cure behind you so that it can strengthen your back and give you a sense of support.

Also, if you are sitting a little low in relation to your tabletop, you may find that you are missing various opportunities and being overlooked. Consider placing a small platform under your chair, raising you to an ergonomically acceptable level in relation to your desk. This platform or dais is a symbol of kingship and confidence, and, even if you don't feel confident at first, and don't feel that you can get the job of your dreams, you will be attracting this kind of energy to you by sitting on your platform, and eventually you will feel able to take control of your life and aim high.

Dealing with stress at work

In feng shui, your career aspiration corresponds to the north section of your home or office and with the area immediately in front of you as you sit at your desk. Stress can occur at work for many reasons, and these reasons fall into one of two broad categories – yang-related and yin-related stress.

Yang-related stress arises from overstimulation of this energy. It can lead to impulsive resignations, argumentativeness, overwork and high absenteeism. This form of stress is prevalent in jobs where a person is required to work all day in front of a computer. As the career section of your desk corresponds to the space immediately in front of you when you are sitting down, positioning your computer in this area may lead to your feeling overworked and tired. This is because computers continually generate a stimulating form of yang energy.

To counter this form of stress, place a yin feature on the right-hand side of the computer, as the right-hand side corresponds to yang energy. Balancing the yin and yang in this area will help rebalance your feelings about your work, and will lead to a rebalancing of your workload.

If you are constantly using your hands and like to wear jewelry, consider wearing a hematite or lapis lazuli ring or bracelet. Hematite is a semiprecious stone that is used by feng shui practitioners for a variety of cures, including the relief of stress.

Yin-related stress occurs when there is a feeling of stagnation about your work. This can have a number of reasons – lack of confidence that you can get the job you want, and feelings of not being valued for what you can really do, for instance. This kind of stress leads to apathy, long drawn-out plans to resign, lack of focus, and poor job performance.

To stimulate the acknowledgment aspiration in feng shui, focus on the southern area of your home and your workplace. On your desk, this area is directly opposite where you sit, near the top of your table or desk. Clear this space and, if required, follow the feng shui cure preparation checklist on page 49.

When you have cleared this area, place a light there that you can keep lit for at least a couple of hours a day. If you work with your back to the door, you may find that your stress levels are heightened. You can cure this by either repositioning your desk so that you can see the entrance or by placing a small mirror in the acknowledgment area so that you can see the entrance while you work. This will not only stimulate positive energy for this aspiration, but also alleviate the stress caused by not facing your entrance.

Carry a piece of white jade to work to attract good luck – jade is an excellent healing stone. You may also consider wearing or carrying some lapis lazuli – this will help alleviate feelings of depression.

HEALTH

Attracting strong life energy

In feng shui there are a number of symbols of longevity that can be incorporated into the home or business – these will stimulate a strong life force that will improve your personal health and increase the odds that your business will survive and flourish. Of course, in feng shui it is important that this energy force is not overwhelmingly strong, as balance is an essential key to the proper beneficial flow of energy.

Images of animals (see page 14) always play an important role in evoking a sense of longevity and endurance. Place pictures or other representations of one of the following creatures in the eastern section of your home to attract long life and good health:

* bat
* cicada
* crane
* deer
* horse
* monkey
* rabbit
* tortoise.

The eastern section of a building corresponds to the family/health aspiration. Focus on this area in the workplace if you wish to improve the longevity and health of your staff.

If you are suffering from an undesired, quick turnover of staff, there may be too much yang or overly strong energy shooting through the workplace. Place a representation of one of the animals on page 66 in this area to encourage a flow of beneficial energy to your staff.

If you find that there are last-minute rushes, poor timing skills and a general sense of apathy in your workplace, there may be too much yin or overly passive energy around, slowing the energy so much that it has become stagnant. Place a piece of citrine unobtrusively in the eastern section of the staff room.

Sometimes, beneficial energy has difficulties reaching your building. The energy may be made to move too fast by the environment around your building so that it approaches your home or business too quickly to add any beneficial stimulation to your life. Placing a screen in the form of a hedge in the garden (see page 34) can counter this fast-moving energy and help to "cure" it.

However, what if the energy in your environment is too yin or passive? You will need to stimulate the energy flow of the environment if you live in a predominantly yin type of house, or if you live next to a predominantly yin environment such as a cemetery, church, rubbish dump or sewage outlet. The flow of energy to you can be aided by placing a bagua (see page 17), with a concave mirror in the middle of it, over your front door, the main entrance through which beneficial energy enters your home.

Clearing ill-health from a sick room

There are two main areas that you need to focus on in the case of ill-health – the bed the person suffering from ill-health is using and the eastern section of your home, which corresponds to the health/family aspiration.

The position of the bed of the ill person is particularly important. Feng shui practitioners believe that an inauspiciously placed bed can have a powerful effect on the health of a person. It is important that the bed is placed in the room so that the person lying in it can see the door. Move the bed if:

* it is under a beam (see also page 30) or below a toilet;
* the headboard shares a common wall with the toilet; or
* the footboard is pointing directly out the door (this is called the "coffin" or "mortuary" position).

Water and life energy are inextricably linked, which is why it is considered inauspicious to place the bed near a toilet, a place where water is made to drain out of the house. In a bedroom, if you can see the toilet from your bed, place a screen (see page 43) between you and the door through which the toilet can be seen.

Remove pictures of rivers, lakes, the sea, and other water features from above the head of the bed, as these are believed to cause or exacerbate ill-health. Also, move the bed if it is directly under a window – this is not considered an auspicious position for a bed.

If possible, place a feng shui cure in the window to attract beneficial energy. These cures include a special five-coin charm that ends with a circular piece of white jade with a hole in the middle. The number five represents the number of the elements (see pages 25–27) and the balance that occurs when all the elements are equally represented.

The presence of mirrors in the bedroom is believed to cause restless sleep and insomnia, therefore it is best to remove or cover mirrors – at least during the period of illness – so that the person can rest and recuperate much more effectively.

The eastern part of the bedroom also corresponds to health. Place all the medicines that are required for the illness in this area. Also include in this area a picture or jade figurine of a cicada, an ancient symbol of longevity and health.

Three gourds can be placed on the ill person's headboard to counter long-term ill-health; and a picture of an elephant, a symbol of strength, can also be included in the sick room to help clear the energy.

Protecting the health of your family

To protect the health of your family, follow the feng shui cure preparation checklist on page 49 to clear the eastern section of your home, which corresponds to the health/family aspiration. Poison arrows and an overly cluttered environment in this area will lead to a series of health problems and family instability. Also focus on the master bedroom, which is the symbol of the head of the family.

It is particularly important to keep the master bedroom clear of clutter and poison arrows, because this bedroom is symbolic of the state of the whole family, including those who grew up in the house but no longer live at home. As a protection against ill-health, clear the eastern part of the master bedroom – or the middle of the wall on the left-hand side of that room as you are looking into the room from the door – and then include an appropriate feng shui cure in either place.

If there is a mirror in this part of the room, remove it or keep it covered. The health/family aspiration resonates with the element of wood, so it is important to remove from this area of the house, and the master bedroom, objects that correspond to the one element that has a destructive relationship with wood – metal. Remove any large metal statues, bowls, or other metal objects, at least for the duration of the problem or ill-health.

If there is already some problem with a family member's health, place an open fan in this section of your home or master bedroom. If you are artistic, you may wish to paint, draw, or even paste an image of a horse (for endurance) or a monkey (for health and protection) on the fan and hang a green tassel, symbolizing health, from one end.

Another place where you can use a feng shui cure to protect your family's health is your bedside tables. These symbolize yang energy (on the right, as you lie in bed) and yin energy (on the left), and they need to be brought back into balance to stimulate the flow of beneficial energy and good health. This can be done in either the master bedroom or in the bedroom of the person who is unwell.

If you have only one bedside table, balance the flow of yin/yang energy by placing two small brass figurines of goats or horses on either side of the bed, perhaps on top of the headboard on each side or on a shelf above your head.

EDUCATION

Attracting success in your coursework

To attract success in your studies, first focus on the places where you spend the majority of your time, such as the bed and your study desk. Clear these areas by following, where appropriate, the feng shui cure preparation checklist on page 49.

The northeast section of your home corresponds to the knowledge aspiration, which needs to be stimulated to attract success and opportunities to study. Feng shui cures that work particularly well in this area relate to color and to the energy generated by the electrical equipment necessary for your work.

To stimulate the knowledge area, it would be best to include rich, vibrant colors that tend toward yang energy, such as reds, oranges, pinks, and yellows. However, do not use these colors indiscriminately – it is important to keep a sense of balance and harmony in the building. It is better to have splashes of bright color enlivening the area.

Overstimulating any area by over-using feng shui cures can create negative energy, which results in more energy flow problems. In this case, the cures merely become clutter, stagnating the energy flow through your home. If you notice a number of feng shui cures as soon as you walk into a room, they are not doing their job of circulating or blending into the flow of energy.

To stimulate the knowledge aspiration, place a red mat in the knowledge area of your home, bedroom or study, and, on top of it, position a statue of the great Chinese philosopher Confucius. If you cannot get a statue, get hold of a color picture of him and place it in a metal frame. This cure can also be placed at the entrance of your home when you need extra support with your studies, such as at exam time. The image at the entrance will infuse the energy flowing through the house.

Similarly, the image of a pagoda is excellent for stimulating success with your studies – some feng shui practitioners recommend that a pagoda image be placed on your bedside table (preferably on the right-hand or yang side of the bed).

If you are seeking to study abroad, consider clearing the northwest section of your house as well – it corresponds to the mentors/travel aspiration. Use the feng shui cure preparation checklist on page 49 and then apply cures to stimulate the energy in this area, such as sound (see page 44) or wind chimes (see page 47). If the area feels stagnant and uninviting, ring a bell in each corner to clear any stagnant energy and leave the windows open when it is sunny to re-energize the area.

Increasing your concentration

To improve your concentration, first clear and organize your work, notes, and assignments so that everything is in a logical place and there is a place for everything you need. To encourage this form of clearing, hang a clear quartz crystal over the desk – its energy will help you eventually clear your space.

If you are finding yourself feeling distracted or unfocused, check that the following do not apply to you:

* your back is facing the entrance; and/or
* you are sitting in an uncomfortable chair.

It is a common feng shui principle that you should never sit with your back to an entrance. This attracts anything from bad luck to feelings of being disturbed in your work (see pages 62–65). Your chair must be comfortable. In feng shui, the most auspicious kind of chair is one that has armrests and a high back – this signifies the support of mountains behind you and symbolically strengthens your spine.

Similarly, hang a picture of mountains behind your chair. An image of a pagoda can also be placed behind your back in the study. The pagoda has a similar energy to a mountain but it symbolizes climbing through levels of expertise. To help you in this advancement of your studies, hang a yellow tassel over your desk.

Crystals are another excellent way to focus your attention (see page 23). If you are in the midst of exams or assignments are due, place a crystal in each corner of your study room. Use crystals such as tiger's eye and fluorite to help you with your studies. Tiger's eye helps clarify your thoughts and fluorite is renowned for its ability to help you retain what you have learnt.

Always remember to clear the space at the end of each project and, if possible, file the information in the knowledge area of your home or office. By taking this information out of your study area, you are symbolically indicating that you wish to move forward with your studies. However, as you are still keeping the necessary files in the knowledge area of your home or workplace, you are retaining the information that you will need in order to successfully continue your studies.

Is this the right course for me?

Finding out whether or not you are doing the right course is a matter of being able to think clearly and work out what you really want from life. Many principles of feng shui are specifically designed so that once a feng shui cure is implemented, your mind is no longer buffeted by negative energies and it will feel clear enough to sort out issues of career path and appropriate studies (see pages 74–75 for feng shui concentration tips).

However, in the Chinese philosophies underlying feng shui principles, it is believed that the elements (see pages 25–27) play a very important part in our ability to understand ourselves. Our year of birth will tell us what our predominant element is. This characteristic governs, among other things, our body type, our personalities, and our preferred modes of work.

In the table opposite you will see that the last digit of your year of birth indicates which element you resonate with, as well as whether you are a yang (assertive) or a yin (passive) aspect of that element. The table also includes what types of work/course best suits each element.

Remember that the Chinese New Year starts at various dates, all of them later than the New Year in the West. The starting dates for the Chinese New Year vary from about January 21 to February 20.

You can use a symbol representing good luck for your element, such as a metal figurine of a rabbit if you were born in the year of the rabbit (see page 15) and in a year ending in the number 1. You could place this symbol in your home, bedroom, workplace, or desk, in a position which corresponds to a particular aspiration (see pages 12–13) that you wish to have stimulated. This is the most personalized feng shui cure of all. You could also carry it with you to attract good luck and fortune.

LAST DIGIT OF YOUR YEAR OF BIRTH	ELEMENT	YIN/YANG	TYPES OF CAREER OR COURSEWORK
0	Metal	Yang	Business Studies, Economics, Law, Politics
1	Metal	Yin	
2	Water	Yang	Philosophy, Arts, Medicine, Writing, Law, Education
3	Water	Yin	
4	Wood	Yang	Science, Computer Programming, Agriculture, Geology
5	Wood	Yin	
6	Fire	Yang	Drama, Psychology, Events Organization, Arts, Journalism
7	Fire	Yin	
8	Earth	Yang	Diplomacy, Psychology, Healing Studies, Architecture
9	Earth	Yin	

Glossary

BAGUA a grid system representing eight aspects of life identified in the I-Ching and applied in the art of feng shui.

CITRINE a yellow stone that can be used for protection.

CHAKRA a series of energy centers running through the middle of the body.

CHI (also known as "qi") the Chinese name for universal energy.

FENG SHUI the Chinese art of placement and design aimed to enhance the flow of universal energy.

I-CHING (also known as the Book of Changes) a complex, lyrical method of divination developed in China many centuries ago.

JADE a green stone that can be used to attract love, wealth, and healing energies. It is also available in white.

LAPIS LAZULI a blue stone with gold pyrite, used to attract wealth and abundance.

POISON ARROW a harmful shaft of energy created by long, straight corridors, paths, or roads, or by sharp angles created by sloping rooflines and vertical objects such as telephone poles.

QI see Chi (above).

YANG male or extrovert energy.

YIN female or introvert energy.

Chinese Calendar

NEW YEAR DATE	ELEMENT	YIN/YANG	FEMALE (E/W)	MALE (E/W)	NEW YEAR DATE	ELEMENT	YIN/YANG	FEMALE (E/W)	MALE (E/W)
1919 FEB 1	EARTH	YIN	WEST	EAST	1964 FEB 13	WOOD	YANG	WEST	EAST
1920 FEB 20	METAL	YANG	WEST	WEST	1965 FEB 2	WOOD	YIN	WEST	WEST
1921 FEB 8	METAL	YIN	WEST	WEST	1966 JAN 21	FIRE	YANG	WEST	WEST
1922 JAN 28	WATER	YANG	EAST	WEST	1967 FEB 9	FIRE	YIN	EAST	WEST
1923 FEB 16	WATER	YIN	EAST	WEST	1968 JAN 30	EARTH	YANG	EAST	WEST
1924 FEB 5	WOOD	YANG	WEST	EAST	1969 FEB 17	EARTH	YIN	WEST	EAST
1925 JAN 24	WOOD	YIN	EAST	EAST	1970 FEB 6	METAL	YANG	EAST	EAST
1926 FEB 13	FIRE	YANG	EAST	WEST	1971 JAN 27	METAL	YIN	EAST	WEST
1927 FEB 2	FIRE	YIN	WEST	EAST	1972 FEB 15	WATER	YANG	WEST	EAST
1928 JAN 23	EARTH	YANG	WEST	EAST	1973 FEB 3	WATER	YIN	WEST	EAST
1929 FEB 10	EARTH	YIN	WEST	WEST	1974 JAN 23	WOOD	YANG	WEST	WEST
1930 JAN 30	METAL	YANG	WEST	WEST	1975 FEB 11	WOOD	YIN	WEST	WEST
1931 FEB 17	METAL	YIN	EAST	WEST	1976 JAN 31	FIRE	YANG	EAST	WEST
1932 FEB 6	WATER	YANG	EAST	WEST	1977 FEB 18	FIRE	YIN	EAST	WEST
1933 JAN 26	WATER	YIN	WEST	EAST	1978 FEB 7	EARTH	YANG	WEST	EAST
1934 FEB 14	WOOD	YANG	EAST	EAST	1979 JAN 28	EARTH	YIN	EAST	EAST
1935 FEB 4	WOOD	YIN	WEST	WEST	1980 FEB 16	METAL	YANG	EAST	WEST
1936 JAN 31	FIRE	YANG	WEST	EAST	1981 FEB 5	METAL	YIN	WEST	EAST
1937 FEB 11	FIRE	YIN	WEST	EAST	1982 JAN 25	WATER	YANG	WEST	EAST
1938 JAN 31	EARTH	YANG	WEST	WEST	1983 FEB 13	WATER	YIN	WEST	WEST
1939 FEB 19	EARTH	YIN	WEST	WEST	1984 FEB 2	WOOD	YANG	WEST	WEST
1940 FEB 8	METAL	YANG	EAST	WEST	1985 FEB 20	WOOD	YIN	EAST	WEST
1941 JAN 27	METAL	YIN	EAST	WEST	1986 FEB 9	FIRE	YANG	EAST	WEST
1942 FEB 18	WATER	YANG	WEST	EAST	1987 JAN 29	FIRE	YIN	WEST	EAST
1943 FEB 5	WATER	YIN	EAST	EAST	1988 FEB 17	EARTH	YANG	EAST	EAST
1944 JAN 25	WOOD	YANG	EAST	WEST	1989 FEB 6	EARTH	YIN	EAST	WEST
1945 FEB 13	WOOD	YIN	WEST	EAST	1990 JAN 27	METAL	YANG	WEST	EAST
1946 FEB 2	FIRE	YANG	WEST	EAST	1991 FEB 15	METAL	YIN	WEST	EAST
1947 JAN 22	FIRE	YIN	WEST	WEST	1992 FEB 4	WATER	YANG	WEST	WEST
1948 FEB 10	EARTH	YANG	WEST	WEST	1993 JAN 23	WATER	YIN	WEST	WEST
1949 JAN 29	EARTH	YIN	EAST	WEST	1994 FEB 10	WOOD	YANG	EAST	WEST
1950 FEB 17	METAL	YANG	EAST	WEST	1995 JAN 31	WOOD	YIN	EAST	WEST
1951 FEB 6	METAL	YIN	WEST	EAST	1996 FEB 19	FIRE	YANG	WEST	EAST
1952 JAN 27	WATER	YANG	EAST	EAST	1997 FEB 7	FIRE	YIN	EAST	EAST
1953 FEB 14	WATER	YIN	EAST	WEST	1998 JAN 28	EARTH	YANG	EAST	WEST
1954 FEB 3	WOOD	YANG	WEST	EAST	1999 FEB 16	EARTH	YIN	WEST	EAST
1955 JAN 24	WOOD	YIN	WEST	EAST	2000 FEB 5	METAL	YANG	WEST	EAST
1956 FEB 12	FIRE	YANG	WEST	WEST	2001 JAN 24	METAL	YIN	WEST	WEST
1957 JAN 31	FIRE	YIN	WEST	WEST	2002 FEB 12	WATER	YANG	WEST	WEST
1958 FEB 18	EARTH	YANG	EAST	WEST	2003 FEB 1	WATER	YIN	EAST	WEST
1959 FEB 8	EARTH	YIN	EAST	WEST	2004 JAN 22	WOOD	YANG	EAST	WEST
1960 JAN 28	METAL	YANG	WEST	EAST	2005 FEB 9	WOOD	YIN	WEST	EAST
1961 FEB 15	METAL	YIN	EAST	EAST	2006 JAN 29	FIRE	YANG	EAST	EAST
1962 FEB 5	WATER	YANG	EAST	WEST	2007 FEB 18	FIRE	YIN	EAST	WEST
1963 JAN 25	WATER	YIN	WEST	EAST	2008 FEB 7	EARTH	YANG	WEST	EAST

This edition published by Barnes & Noble, Inc.,
by arrangement with Lansdowne Publishing

First published 2002
Reprinted 2002, 2003
M 10 9 8 7 6 5 4 3

ISBN 0-7607-3235-3

Commissioned by Deborah Nixon
Text: Antonia Beattie
Illustrator: Tina Wilson, with additional illustrations by Penny Lovelock,
Sue Ninham and Jane Cameron
Cover illustration: Tina Wilson
Designer: Avril Makula
Editor: Sarah Shrubb
Production Manager: Jane Kirby
Project Co-ordinator: Kate Merrifield

Set in Orange and Stone Serif on Quark XPress
Printed in Singapore by Tien Wah Press (Pte) Ltd